How To Find All Missing Persons / Unsolved Cases. And Collect All Reward Offers. Volume XXXXVII THE CASE OF AS IT HAPPENS

DAVID GOMADZA

www.twofuture.world

How To Find All Missing Persons / Unsolved Cases. And
Collect All Reward Offers. Volume XXXXVII. THE CASE OF AS IT HAPPENS

Copyright © 2024 David Gomadza

All rights reserved.

Paperback ISBN: 9798329134971

How To Find All Missing Persons / Unsolved Cases. And
Collect All Reward Offers. Volume XXXXVII. THE CASE OF AS IT HAPPENS

DEDICATION

To a better future.

How To Find All Missing Persons / Unsolved Cases. And
Collect All Reward Offers. Volume XXXXVII. THE CASE OF AS IT HAPPENS

How To Find All Missing Persons / Unsolved Cases. And
Collect All Reward Offers. Volume XXXXVII. THE CASE OF AS IT HAPPENS

CONTENTS

How To Find All Missing Persons /
Unsolved Cases.
And Collect All Reward Offers. Volume XXXXVII
THE CASE OF AS IT HAPPENS 1
Conversation.

The Perfect Orphans Laws and Their Rights to Their

Own Property. Extracts from the Book of Creation.

How To Find All Missing Persons / Unsolved Cases. And
Collect All Reward Offers. Volume XXXXVII. THE CASE OF AS IT HAPPENS

How To Find All Missing Persons / Unsolved Cases. And
Collect All Reward Offers. Volume XXXXVII. THE CASE OF AS IT HAPPENS

ACKNOWLEDGMENTS

Tomorrow's World Order

How To Find All Missing Persons / Unsolved Cases. And
Collect All Reward Offers. Volume XXXXVII. THE CASE OF AS IT HAPPENS

How To Find All Missing Persons / Unsolved Cases. And Collect All Reward Offers. Volume XXXXVII. THE CASE OF AS IT HAPPENS

How To Find All Missing Persons / Unsolved Cases. And Collect All Reward Offers. Volume XXXXVII THE CASE OF AS IT HAPPENS

BACKGROUND INFORMATION

We know a lot about this $1 million police syndicate and the housing scam from the cases of Revelle Balmin-smith and Janine Vaughan where Pc aterop ares said I quote;

*pc aterop ares said to him we want both these ladies dead i am telling you as your boss not as a policemen today we need to get rid of these cheeky ladies forever okay so this is what you do ask to wait for me if she runs away then leave her she will have given you the respect you deserve but if not then grab her neck and fill your dick inside her cummings inside her that feeling you would kill for right because i would kill for to you to be eaten by you after great sex i would love that so can we come when you are having a great time or you have a great time first then we come after to kill you and send you to them as r that now just imagine the best virgin in town coming well because you too now know too much so we might as well kill you just **imagine someone knowing that surely he will break lose the whole police force will be destroyed that we pray on the weak but rich for their property this is true because i want janine's house for 20 dollars and pc aers want Revelle's house** so we teamed up and make sure that we kill all today and swap their houses then send the documents to the police housing association and then take the houses for ourselves then sell all in 5 years for 2* million that's being clever so if we can we can do this now or wait when we are 60 to enjoy more money in the police where rewards top up our millionaire accounts for the next 100 years without a single human being able to solve any case but only god even if he did we can actually hide his evidence or swap it around unless he is to publish as books that he can use later to prove we steal without this then we are safe but then again where us god people were looking for god for years above all we can divert that send.ya to ourselves now using a simple code 08923678902867890289038678901 that means that Yahweh will always be there but we are now the people's god the reason why the force is doing this is to be able to stand the pressure for change and returning of these houses since 1948 as i understand this is the year this began in europe due to the 1948 convention of human rights that took away powers used by the queen to take property from orphans who would eventually lose the property through an underground operation termed then capital gains tax verdict act that was hidden but operated everywhere the first reason police took part in this scam is that they believed they gain as well free house for 20 and 1 million guaranteed at age 60 of retirement through the use of other accounts to receive money the accounts are synchronized to real accounts through a chip system that says ask.ya.620 this send all your funds to one place and you will get a notification when done that says you received cash from a source this source is the consolidation system of the police who send money to hide accounts once that is done then this credited to your accounts the next day in real times when you check your accounts then you will see real money

This is how this is done
1. They find the killer for the orphans yet rich in this case Janine and Revelle
2. They prey on the weak for their houses they can easily choose and buy for a 20 dollar bill.
3. They team up for a kill get their houses and swap them then send them to the housing association

4. then take the houses for themselves then sell all in 5 years for 2 million dollars that's being clever

5. enjoy more money in the police where rewards top up our millionaire accounts for the next 100 years without a single human being able to solve any case but only god even if he did we can actually hide his evidence or swap it around unless he is to publish as books that he can use later to prove we steal.

This is proof that rewards for the next 100 years is part of a $1 million prize reward scheme and why 100 years

This is also proof that these cases are not meant to be solved because they will keep swapping evidence and hiding evidence until the reward prize has reached maturity.

That means that joining the force will guarantee a police officer a free house for $20 and 1 million guaranteed at age 60 of retirement through the use of other accounts to receive money the accounts are synchronized to real accounts through a chip system that says ask.ya.620

But how do this reward system work?

First let's look at the case of Pauline Sowry where the death by codes squad of the police grouped to kill this boys mother.. .and she fell asleep and quickly pc asert pc asoper pc aotmny gathered and said if he can why can't we did he tried to kill his mum and they all looked at each other and said i can if you can then joined hands and said then after 2 we do the same exact date and reposes the house for pc artoper who said i want to live in this house but then left the force so after two years we offer him this precious house to him for 20 dollars so we are back again the way we were now gentlemen let's take her to Ya so these are tasks for today to be successful so that we can't get caught

Pc artoper had left the force because he couldn't get someone's house that he left such as a person cherished by his friends they are driven to kill the rightful owner a helpless mother with her son death now for the mother and death for the son the next year

All this so that they invite their colleague who left because he wanted the house.

Police stealing money

Proof of how the police steal real money from the orphans these are the same cops who forced the receiving bank account of the mother to be closed the day it received life insurance money from the insurance company for her husband who killed himself at work then transferred a chunk to the police bank account:
transferred [to son] 2500 dollars enough to cover for 1 year
mum and then sent 700 to the lover knowing they killed him already by digital blinding while at the wheel
they sent 287680 to their own police bank account all this money was hibernating in her account from the death of her husband a few months ago when he pretended to go away and went to die at work and saying don't tell my wife but just send the check if she know i died then she would kill herself but the day it was deposited the police froze her account and she said if there was money then i would fight for this account and

EXTRACTED FROM

The Perfect Orphans Laws and Their Rights to Their Own Property.Extracts from the Book of Creation.

https://play.google.com/store/books/details/David_Gomadza_The_Perfect_Orphans_Laws_and_Their_R?id=ZtoPEQAAQBAJ

How To Find All Missing Persons / Unsolved Cases. And Collect All Reward Offers. Volume XXXXVII. THE CASE OF AS IT HAPPENS

TOMORROW'S WORLD ORDER'S PERSPECTIVES

FINDING SOLUTIONS

1. We can ask other independent bodies to complete one stage of the process this can be a bank or building society that can check ownership and make sure that all the rules are adhered to but only according to the predefined system parameters these must put signatures as well on the documents saying that the police have followed all the procedures and are acting within the law I think it is a bad thing for the police to take the law into their own hands if we look at this this way then you can easily tell that something is out of the ordinarily and will always be critical when deciding what to do in these situations if we are correct then we can say that we can always ask if you are doing the right thing because as predefined parameters we can always know when to start and stop this means that we can issue everything to everyone then go there and ask what can be done if nothing can be done then one has to ask oneself what can be done in these situations if nothing then we move on to the nearest point and ask these questions again until nothing can be done then we do the same so now to create such predefined stencils we need to understand the context in which all these occur most they occur under duress when a police officer start to admire property that belongs to others then that's a problem if we look at such a case we can look at the case that happened today in Canada where a police officer in the pretense of collecting capital gains taxes tricked a teenager to change her name today so that it's easy to claim back her house but in actual fact make it worse to claim back all this because he liked the house and has asked others to pretend to like the house so that there is bidding among the police this is the case between aspen ire who said today I got tricked by someone I trusted all my life for my own

house that has nothing to do with the law but shear love of the property of others well-endowed in property I must change back this as soon as possible there are talks of God intervening everywhere so where is this God today I prayed all night to guide me but I did not hear him say anything there are stories in Mexico where God intervened and rescued a boy injured in the forest literally asking him to take away his pain and link him to his father even though the father turned out to be the enemy now if we look at this case then we can see the dirty tactics police use

1. They lie and unlawfully force the orphan to change his or her name just past 15 years old most on false or unsupported charges that make it unrealistic for orphans to deal with the law when about to claim the house if we look at this then we can always say if we look at this in this way then no kid can be tricked ever again we must include predefined settings in the system where both the police officer and the orphan involved are and must meet certain regulations to make sure that all is within the law the teen must always refuse and ask an independent body to stand for him instead before changing his or her name they make dirty deals because there are no safeguards to protect orphans from being tricked often with time frames for example nothing can happen at the same time the suggestion name change should be announce first followed by consultation by a third party and weeks later if within the law and all rules put in place for an automatic revert to original name 3 months before the collection of the house

This is critical because this will safeguard that when the house is due to be handed back then all the papers are in good form all names on identification documents matches those on the house

2. The police lie about the real reason for wanting the property all lie that it's to protect capital gains taxes if it's for capital gains taxes then they can't stay in that house this should be part of the predefined parameter in that they must not personally associate themselves with the property they are taking or their close friends in most cases they play syndicates in which they rotate the wheel of fortune and also rotate the turns for themselves and their friends

this is easily avoidable by predefining this outright and have strict laws and punishment that says that if there is a problem then this is how to solve it now let's look at two critical issues regarding enforcing this

1. Police business is none of others business they are the only ones that can breach laws and still walk away in that by the time it might come to light of what is happening it might be too late you must always make sure that there are things that need checking as in ticking a box that can't be disclosed therefore there must be a third party to report to and turn to for clarification when the thieving policy decides that they want to take a property unlawfully if we look at what is happening in remote areas of Canada, Australia, England then you can see that the police have gone one step in the wrong direction targeting the rich and reduce them to rabble then take everything good they have to some even their money which they jam and force the bank to close the account and then try and withdraw the funds themselves now what can we do in such situations we can always ask what can be done and when then know what are our possibilities we can always ask other people to come to the rescue and take things to the better side we can always ask what is to be done then this is the answer we can always do what is right when it comes to things like asking the right questions if we are to proceed with this then what else must we look at and how is this so if we can then what can be done we must check all the possible options available then be ready to call for help if necessary if we look at what can be done then we can easily ask an independent advisor to verify everything we do we must be in a position to ask if there are things we can do then what are they and how can we accomplish these once that is answered then we can be ready to move on to the next step to make sure that there is nothing else we must do to make sure that the next stage is completed as fully as possible looking at all options once that is completed we can look at other things we must do to make sure that the orphan is fully aware of what must be done and how that can be done

How To Find All Missing Persons / Unsolved Cases. And Collect All Reward Offers. Volume XXXXVII. THE CASE OF AS IT HAPPENS

EXTRACTED FROM

The Perfect Orphans Laws and Their Rights to Their Own Property.Extracts from the Book of Creation.

https://play.google.com/store/books/details/David_Gomadza_The_Perfect_Orphans_Laws_and_Their_R?id=ZtoPEQAAQBAJ

CONVERSATION

my name is ...... and i am 16 today and i lost my name today in a freaky accident where police officer stortet said i have made a mistake and wrote your name as ... meaning ...
   meaning .... instead of .... so you will need to change your papers before you collect the house when you become 18 but you can change now but you will lose the benefit of living a free life in the dorms of the college campus and i got upset and said i will change today later and i went to the office with the documents and they said you must change tomorrow but it's closed change monday then i said okay my dad was .... and he died young and we had just moved from ottawa where mum died he sold his house and bought a smaller for 878924678 from 2890867890286 he was literally a billionaire who had gold deposits and was a banker as well people envied him until he got cancer and died crying so much i never thought man can cry but it's life today i was suspended from college because i had not paid fees i cant access my dad's accounts but he had life insurance as well the police said they will look into it but been 8 months now still nothing but food only i phoned the company where he used to work and they said he left nothing for me he took everything with him so i am stuck but it could be worse the police are helping but it could be worse

daddy
my name is .. meaning …. i was the richest person in america by far then moved to australia to look for gold and in 1986 i struck gold and became one of the most influential people in the world and bought the biggest house in ottawa and asked people what life could be then i received a code that said you lost everything but you have me then i saw a man standing outside and he said if i knew it was you then i would not have sold my gold to you because the curse will come to you eventually and he disappeared i turned and looked and he was not there anymore then it started as a migraine then it went to headaches then shivers then i lost erection then the ability to ask then everything stopped then i started hearing things making noises then i said i can hear you talk and it said we ara 1
long ago 8 seconds reduced to 6 then 4 then 2 then let's go home take his falling parts said one and then another said if you can then ask what can be and one said you could be in hell for eternity but your wealth saved you you gave orphans that's all it took and he said okay and left today then he said go in peace and as i look at him he looked like the devil but in white so i said what the fuck is going here then he said i can't be asked today i heard you are coming to today all long ago stopped today meaning only your could be heard god sometimes brings superstars so that he can publicize their good work but he said i can but then walked away then he said if i had my powers i could have sent you back people like you make me want to recreate again of all people it's only you who understood that to find god is to look for gold i live forever where the greatest amounts of gold deposits are and its not far from where you find yours these are my coordinates and whispered them to me and literally saw the coordinates floating …….
…………
then he said if i could appoint a representative i would have liked someone who loves gold i am gold my life is gold you are me in disguise for everything i standard for is gold but gold then gold and

gold and more gold then gold and more gold and gold and gold and gold then i vanished and cried like a baby then closed my eyes

my name is ... today officer pc asortensert said i want to make sure that that i can trust you and you can trust me because i feel you want to give the house to pc aersot for safe keeping until you are 18 then collect but he is a junior to me i have 8 houses i look after for others bit yours is the most expensive i got valuation today from aerstert meaning sorest valuations and estate management who said i can if you can then he said if i can but then and what then drop dead then i take for sure by the 08th of october 2024 at 18.00pm canada time then i said okay you take but i won't be 18 it's only then calculated the coordinates and they became money when i looked at them and said did i just see money what did i ask then him again but he said it's too expensive [using tricks code 08923678902846789084]
i am pc steropstert i am the officer in charge of capital gains tax but in other words enriching us until we die then wait for retirement age when a bonus is added of all rewards because can a apart from australia has the greatest number of rewards per state they have 8 states but their cold cases rack in 64 million per state multiplied by 8 that is 512 million per year money from the treasury who are former cops and the deputies who all have secret accounts all to the tunes of 800 million dollars but all still not collected because if this gets out we are all finished because it's all state money used to fund these cold cases it's not like in australia where they send in donations from the people where missuse can be let to happen without any recuperation if we look at all these cold cases then we can see a pattern imaging they all follow a pattern they are in such a way that once you use evidence from one that removes all similar that means that if we remove one case and payout someone for real then all 63 left are automatically locked that means the more we give out the more we lock as well as an incentive unlike the fbi that has never given a penny
if we ask what happened then this is the answer he contacted god

and said can i ask you a few questions and she said god i died this is the worrying part because he did not answer in denial to say that i am not god but listened and wrote and said add then stopped this is the language of angels but which ones good or bad
my name is steropserot meaning steronopt i am a cop with the canadian death squad we are the ones who are sent to kill orphans literally through what we call lethal injection but codes that imitates anything i am lethal since i qualified no one has ever attempted to upset me but it's boring i tell you but recently we have had a run of our money as the most feared man has arisen among us but he don't know how to play but i think it has not sunk in because he did not announce as expected we heard the british are fighting him pretending everything on earth but we know why he took them several times to court but with no luck but started reading and realised that the british say only god can judge me so he embarked on a journey to look for god but not sure what happened then we heard god has been found but he escaped unannounced then we realise he doesn't know anything at all what must happen he must ask everyone to return stolen ....

…….i am only 16 years today but i start then at top but today i was tricked by aseropt who said if we can't keep the house then what's the use then you can be of any help if you can go to hell but you have to live try everything first like reason with her that death is 2 months away no one has ever escaped this treatment ever because it steady as death because it's the only lethal around you defeat this then you will leave we never chase after but everyone is saying god if it's true he is here can here people enough to defend them then this is the test and how strong he is the time has come for the fight between good and evil and he must ask the right questions to get everything out in the open like where is this
my name is ..meaning .. i have a life insurance policy with ….. but my daughter only access the money at the age of 17 on 18 of march 2025 according to the will with ……… meaning …….. meaning ….. who is my ex wife but God i think said she once came back and sent

her for rebirth last year her full name is ....
but she has a husband now the police agreed they leave the house alone and instead go and fuck themselves in hell if this representative comes then he must send all to help first day before they release codes to kill my daughter for the house i said i am best buddy with *God* i once came here with liquor and he said what are you doing too much liquor call for god to see what you created and what's you are doing i laughed and i woke up back on earth he sent me back ny a simple command
she can ask this god's representative and get him killed because he keep asking

i died on 28 may 2024 at the beach looking in the skies i just said i am so tired i haven't slept for two days then i saw an opposing star and it said why not
...

i died god i was very sick something ate everything and i died it was the most wrenching death i have suffered the first one was better than this one and god said i told you when you cheat death things multiply forever even i sent you again this time will be worse than before that's how life works otherwise it would have been easy but then again and he gave a code and said here is a code but when my representative comes he will send you for rebirth with his predefined parameters as mine are not for humans and will always repel see why humans cant leave forever we are not compatible so when is he coming then he said he found me but i don't know much about him the code is ..
.... with his own predefined parameters
i am pc sterop i am sent to kill you and break a record starting 17 july and kill you

THE POTENTIAL KILLERS THE CONFESSIONS AND THE COORDINATES

i am pc sterop i am sent to kill you and break a record starting 17 july 2024 and kill you

Potential aseropt

i am pc steropstert i am the officer in charge of capital gains tax but in other words enriching us until we die then wait for retirement age when a bonus is added of all rewards because can a apart from australia has the greatest number of

...I found God...visit www.twofuture.world

How To Find All Missing Persons / Unsolved Cases. And Collect All Reward Offers. Volume XXXXVII. THE CASE OF AS IT HAPPENS

THE CLAIM

the reward offer

THE COLLECTION

www.twofuture.world/donate

ABOUT DAVID GOMADZA

visit www.twofuture.world

signed david gomadza
ask.davidgomadzaauthorised.licensed.checkya.askya.ya

22 June 2024 00.30 am
scotland
00447719210295
davidgomadza@hotmail.com
info@twofuture.world

www.ingramcontent.com/pod-product-compliance
Lightning Source LLC
Chambersburg PA
CBHW031518210526
45464CB00007B/2975